INVASIVE SPECIES

BURMESE PYTHONS

by Alicia Z. Klepeis

pogo

Ideas for Parents and Teachers

Pogo Books let children practice reading informational text while introducing them to nonfiction features such as headings, labels, sidebars, maps, and diagrams, as well as a table of contents, glossary, and index.

Carefully leveled text with a strong photo match offers early fluent readers the support they need to succeed.

Before Reading

- "Walk" through the book and point out the various nonfiction features. Ask the student what purpose each feature serves.
- Look at the glossary together. Read and discuss the words.

Read the Book

- Have the child read the book independently.
- Invite him or her to list questions that arise from reading.

After Reading

- Discuss the child's questions. Talk about how he or she might find answers to those questions.
- Prompt the child to think more. Ask: Burmese pythons are some of the world's biggest snakes. Can you name any other large animals?

Pogo Books are published by Jump!
5357 Penn Avenue South
Minneapolis, MN 55419
www.jumplibrary.com

Library of Congress Cataloging-in-Publication Data

Names: Klepeis, Alicia, 1971- author.
Title: Burmese pythons / by Alicia Z. Klepeis.
Description: Minneapolis, MN: Jump!, Inc., [2023]
Series: Invasive species | Includes index.
Audience: Ages 7-10
Identifiers: LCCN 2021058626 (print)
LCCN 2021058627 (ebook)
ISBN 9781636907864 (hardcover)
ISBN 9781636907871 (paperback)
ISBN 9781636907888 (ebook)
Subjects: LCSH: Burmese python—Juvenile literature.
Classification: LCC QL666.O63 K57 2023 (print)
LCC QL666.O63 (ebook) | DDC 597.96/78—dc23/eng/20211201
LC record available at https://lccn.loc.gov/2021058626
LC ebook record available at https://lccn.loc.gov/2021058627

Editor: Eliza Leahy
Designer: Michelle Sonnek

Photo Credits: dwi putra stock/Shutterstock, cover, 8, 18; Rosa Jay/Shutterstock, 1, 23; dwi putra/Alamy, 3; Heiko Kiera/Shutterstock, 4, 5; Nigel Hicks/Alamy, 6-7; Teo Tarras/Shutterstock, 9; Utopia_88/iStock, 10-11; Richard A McMillin/Shutterstock, 12-13 (top); Jack Nevitt/Shutterstock, 12-13 (bottom); Warren Metcalf/Shutterstock, 14-15tl; godi photo/Shutterstock, 14-15tr; Don Mammoser/Shutterstock, 14-15bl, 20-21; Russell Marshall/Shutterstock, 14-15br; Paul Tessier/Shutterstock, 16-17; Joe Raedle/Getty, 19.

Printed in the United States of America at Corporate Graphics in North Mankato, Minnesota.

TABLE OF CONTENTS

CHAPTER 1

ON THE HUNT

Imagine you are in the Florida Everglades. **Wetlands** are all around. A giant snake swims by. Its colors and pattern blend in. It is a Burmese python!

The snake blends in on land, too. It hunts for **prey**.

The python sticks out its tongue. This helps it **sense** prey.

When the prey comes near, the snake strikes fast! Its jaws open wide. Its sharp teeth grip its prey. The snake's body **coils** around it. The animal cannot breathe. It dies. The python swallows it whole. *Gulp!*

DID YOU KNOW?

Burmese pythons can be 23 feet (7.0 meters) long. They can weigh 200 pounds (91 kilograms). That is more than most adults!

tongue

CHAPTER 2

PYTHON PROBLEMS

Burmese pythons are **native** to southeast Asia. They live in jungles and **marshes** there. They live in similar **habitats** in the southeastern United States. The snakes are an **invasive species** in this area.

A Burmese python was first seen in Florida in 1979. How did it get there? It may have been a pet that escaped. Or its owners may have set it free. Other pet Burmese pythons must have made their way into the wild, too.

These snakes can travel long distances. They swim well. This likely helped them spread. It could help them spread even farther.

TAKE A LOOK!

Where have Burmese pythons been found in the United States? Take a look!

Burmese pythons put native **predators** at risk. How? They hunt the same animals. They share habitat, too. Alligators and Florida panthers are two examples.

DID YOU KNOW?

Scientists think Burmese pythons could **adapt** to live in other habitats, such as forests.

alligator

Florida panther

bobcat

fox

raccoon

wood stork

Burmese pythons mostly eat small **mammals** and birds. But they can also eat big prey like deer. They hunt bobcats and foxes. They also eat raccoons and wood storks. This has reduced the **populations** of these animals.

Burmese pythons can live up to 25 years. That gives them a lot of time to produce young.

A female can lay up to 100 eggs at a time. She wraps her body around them. This protects the eggs from predators. It also keeps them warm. After the snakes hatch, the mom leaves. The young snakes are on their own.

DID YOU KNOW?

Newborn Burmese pythons can be up to 24 inches (61 centimeters) long. That is longer than a newborn human! Their large size protects them from predators.

egg

CHAPTER 3

TAKING ACTION

Scientists try to stop Burmese pythons from spreading. But it is difficult. Their **camouflage** makes them hard to find.

Some dogs are trained to find the snakes. Scientists safely catch the snakes. Then, the snakes are **euthanized**. This helps keep the snake population from growing.

Burmese pythons are amazing snakes. But Florida is not their natural home. Alligators, birds, and other native animals will survive better without them.

ACTIVITIES & TOOLS

TRY THIS!

FLORIDA'S SNAKES

Burmese pythons are not the only snakes in Florida. Learn about Florida's native snakes in this activity!

What You Need:

- books, magazines, or a computer
- sheets of paper
- colored pencils, markers, or crayons
- glue or tape
- posterboard or a large sheet of paper

1. **Use books, magazines, or a computer to learn about snakes that are native to the Florida Everglades. Choose two.**
2. **Find out how big the snakes get and what they look like.**
3. **On a sheet of paper, draw one of the snakes. Record how big it gets.**
4. **Repeat Step 3 for the other snake.**
5. **Glue or tape your drawings to your posterboard or large sheet of paper.**
6. **What are some similarities between the native snakes you researched and Burmese pythons? What are some differences?**

GLOSSARY

adapt: To change to fit a different situation.

camouflage: A disguise or natural coloring that allows animals to hide by making them look like their surroundings.

coils: Winds or wraps around something.

euthanized: Put to death in a humane manner.

habitats: The places where animals or plants are usually found.

invasive species: Any kind of living organism that is not native to a specific area.

mammals: Warm-blooded animals that have hair or fur and usually give birth to live babies.

marshes: Areas of wet, muddy land.

native: Growing or living naturally in a particular area of the world.

populations: The total numbers of living things in certain areas.

predators: Animals that hunt other animals for food.

prey: Animals that are hunted by other animals for food.

sense: To feel or become aware of something.

wetlands: Areas of land where there is a lot of moisture in the soil.

INDEX

TO LEARN MORE

Finding more information is as easy as 1, 2, 3.

1. Go to www.factsurfer.com
2. Enter "Burmesepythons" into the search box.
3. Choose your book to see a list of websites.

FACT SURFER